Libro de Colorear

Poneys

Coloring Pages for Kids

Coloring Pages for Kids
An imprint of Ciparum LLC

Libro de Colorear Poneys
© 2017 Ciparum LLC
All rights reserved.
ISBN-10:1-63589-407-7
ISBN-13:978-1-63589-407-3

Coloring Pages for Kids

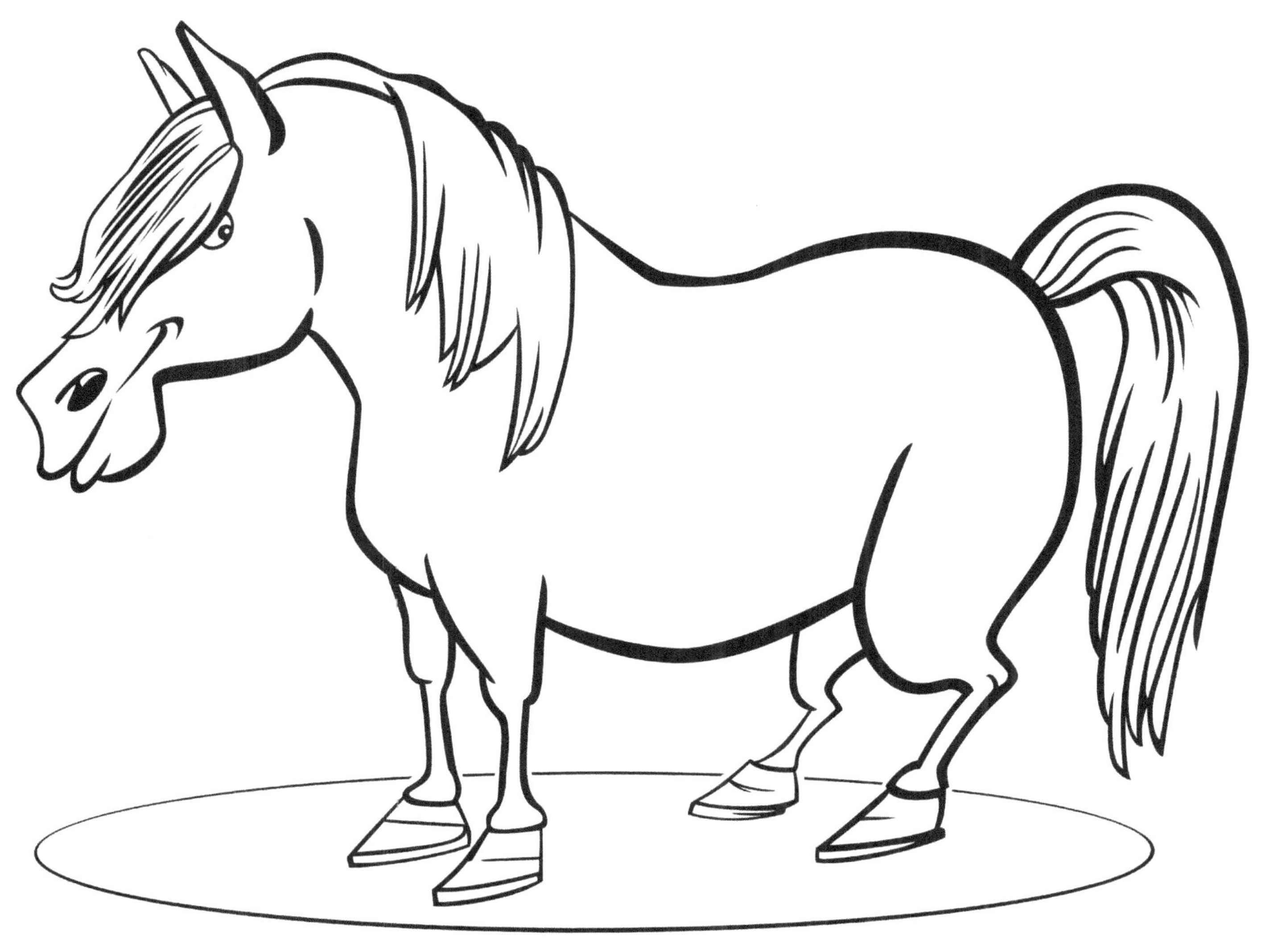

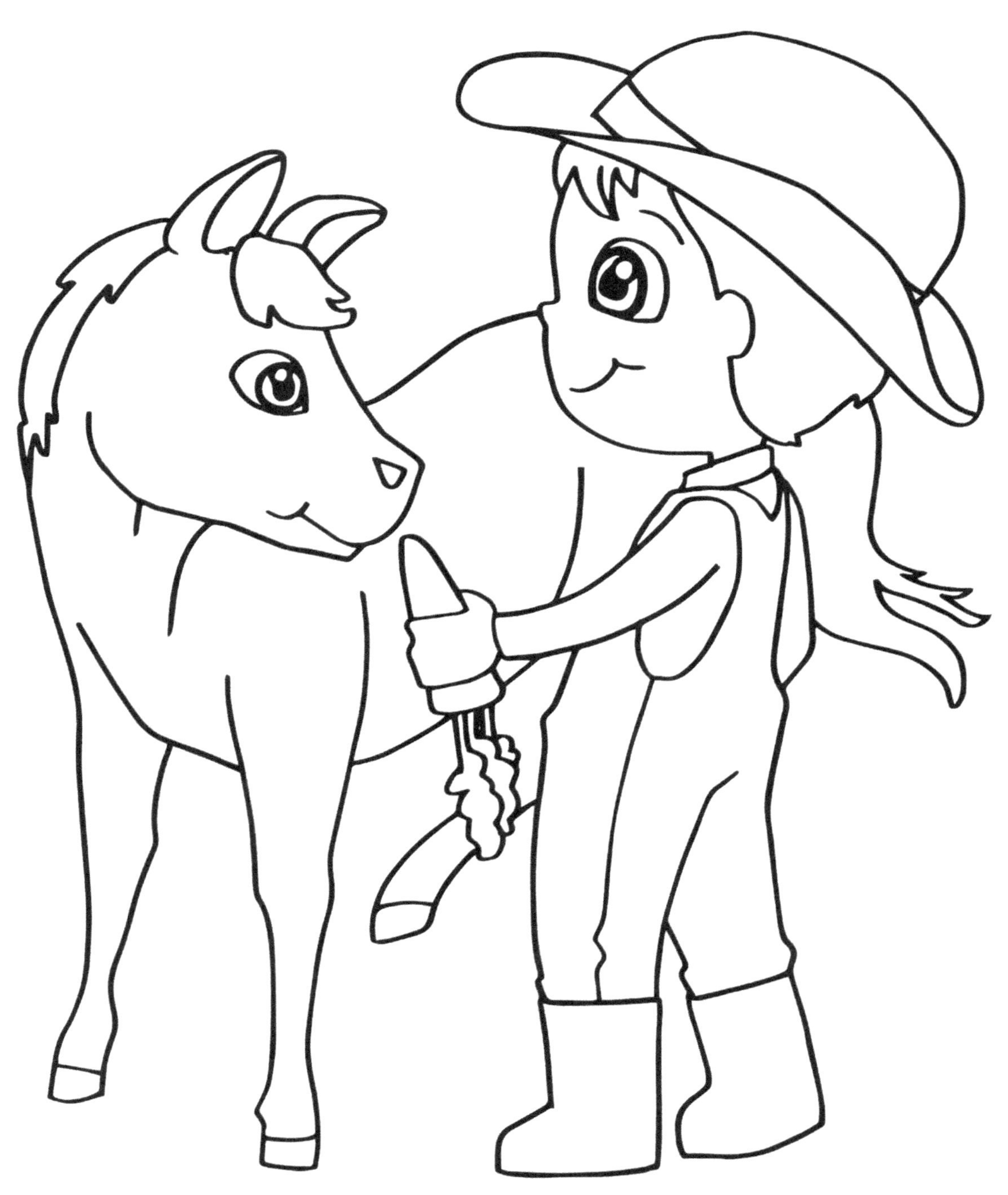

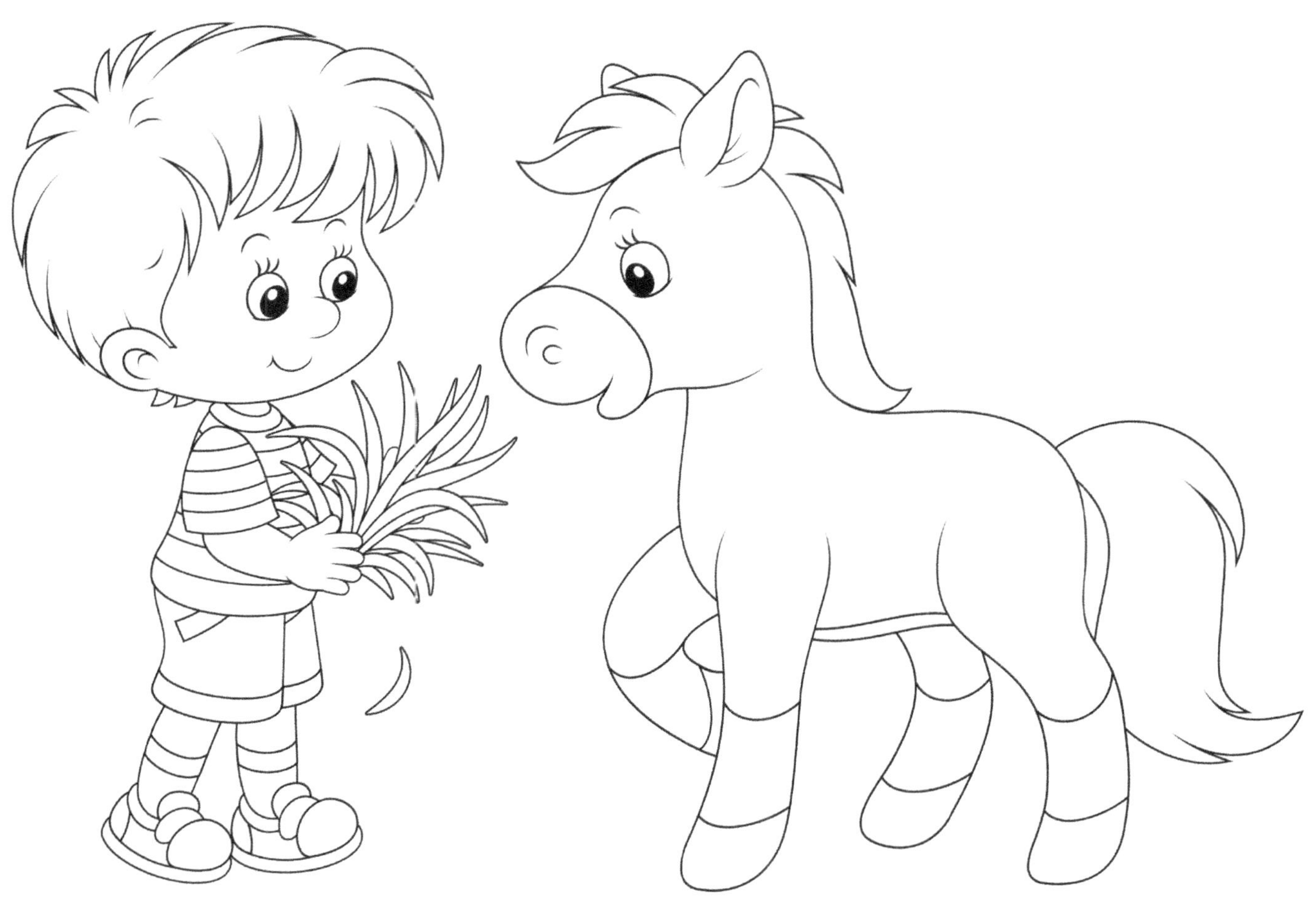

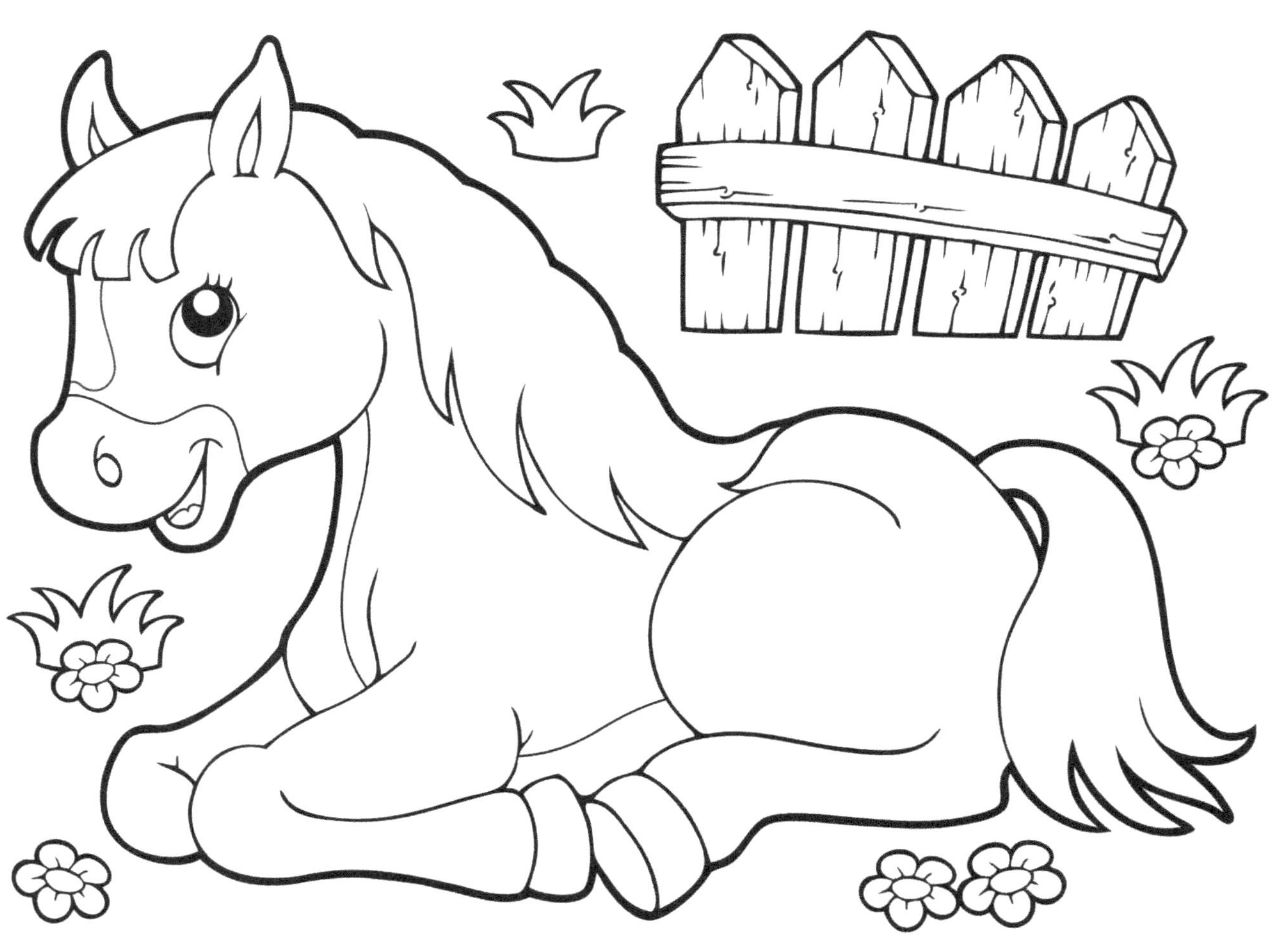

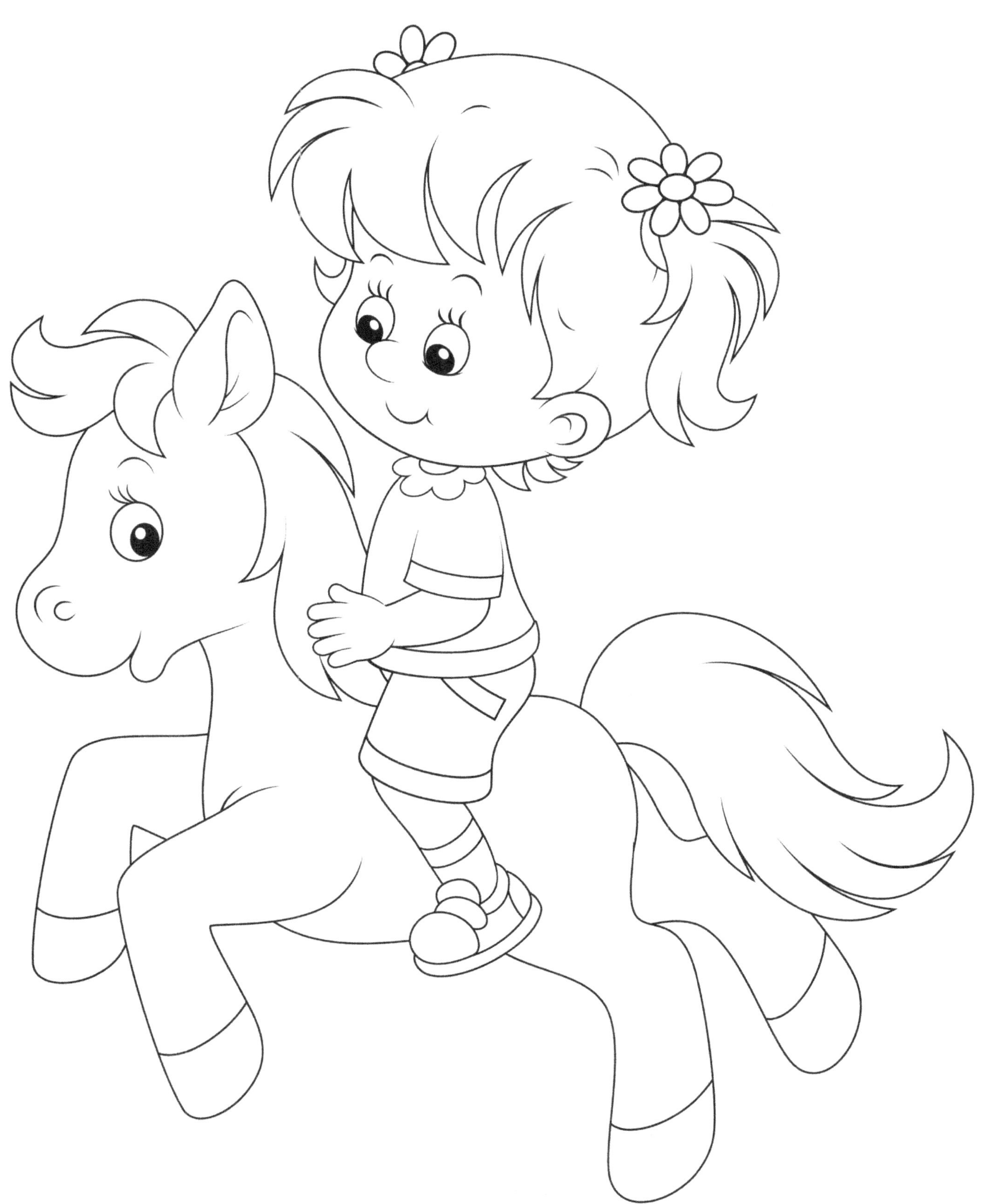

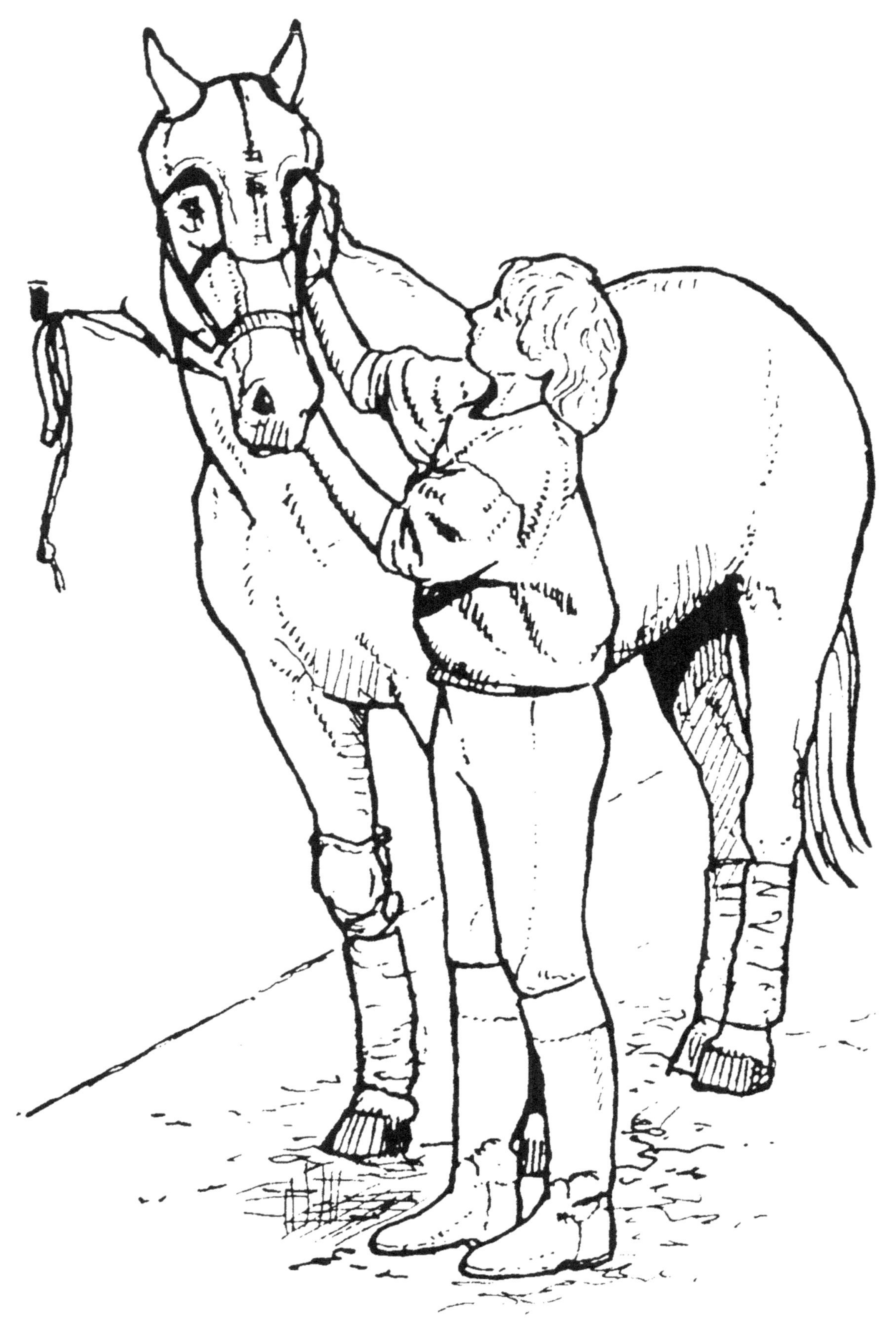

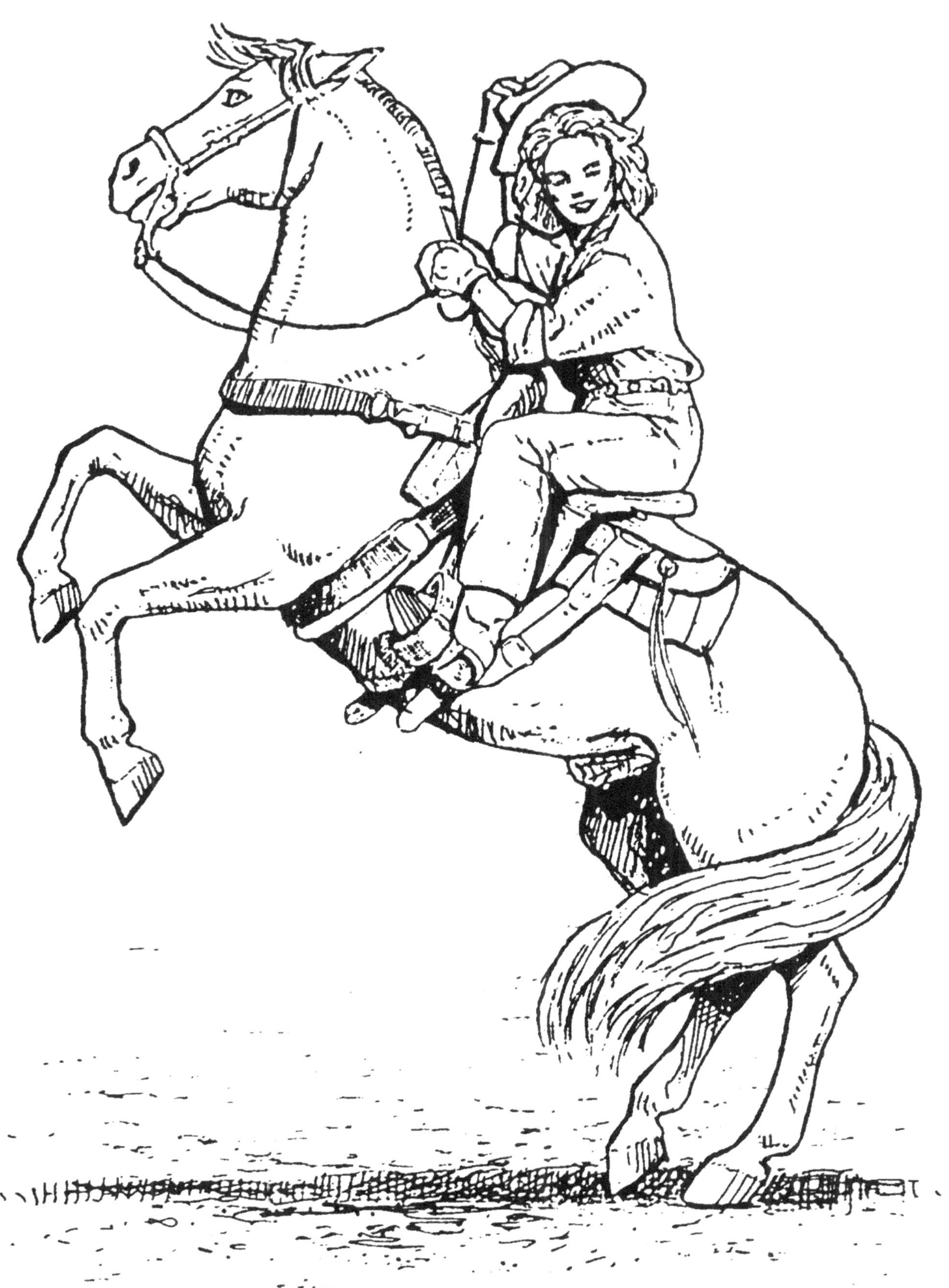

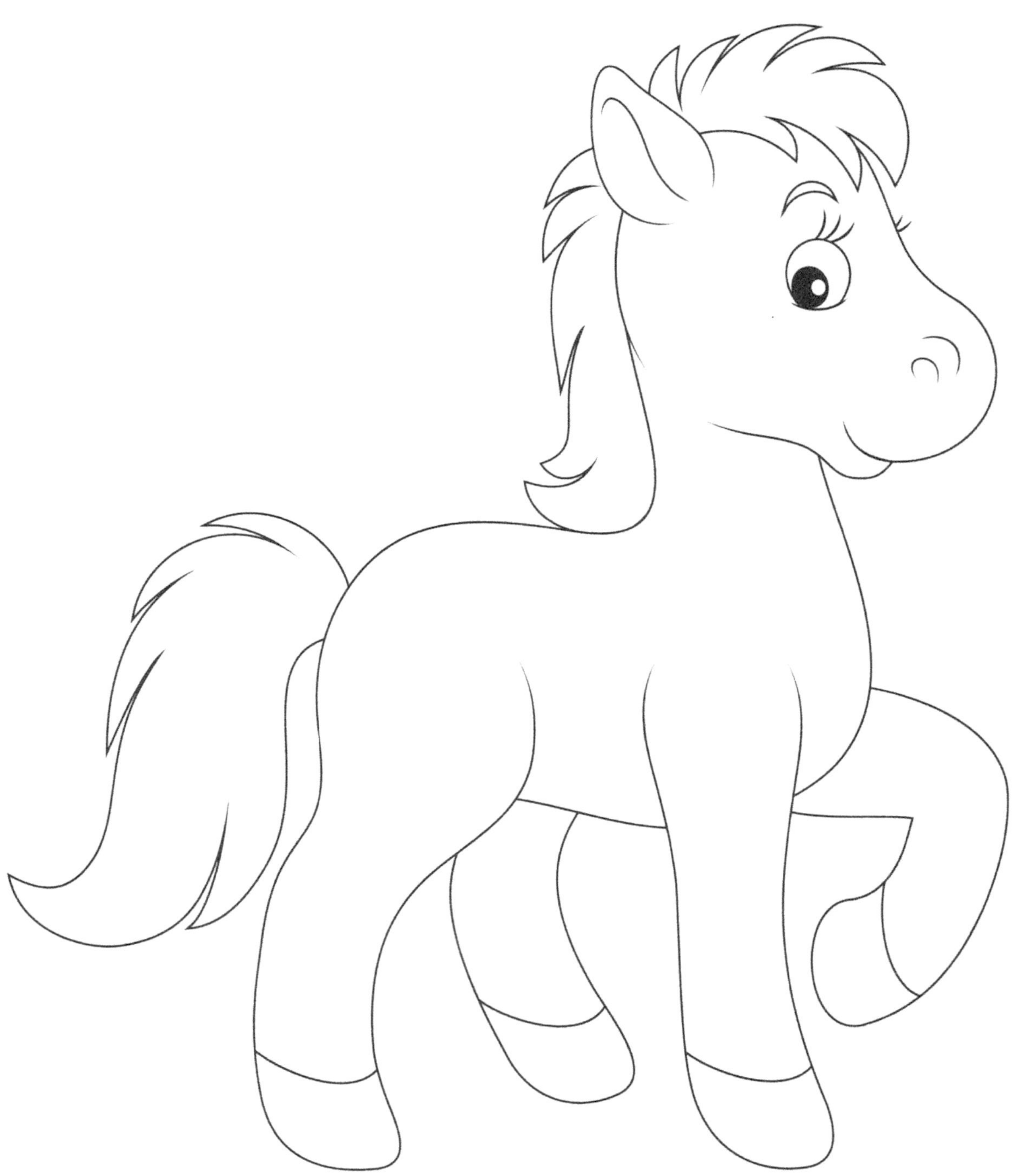

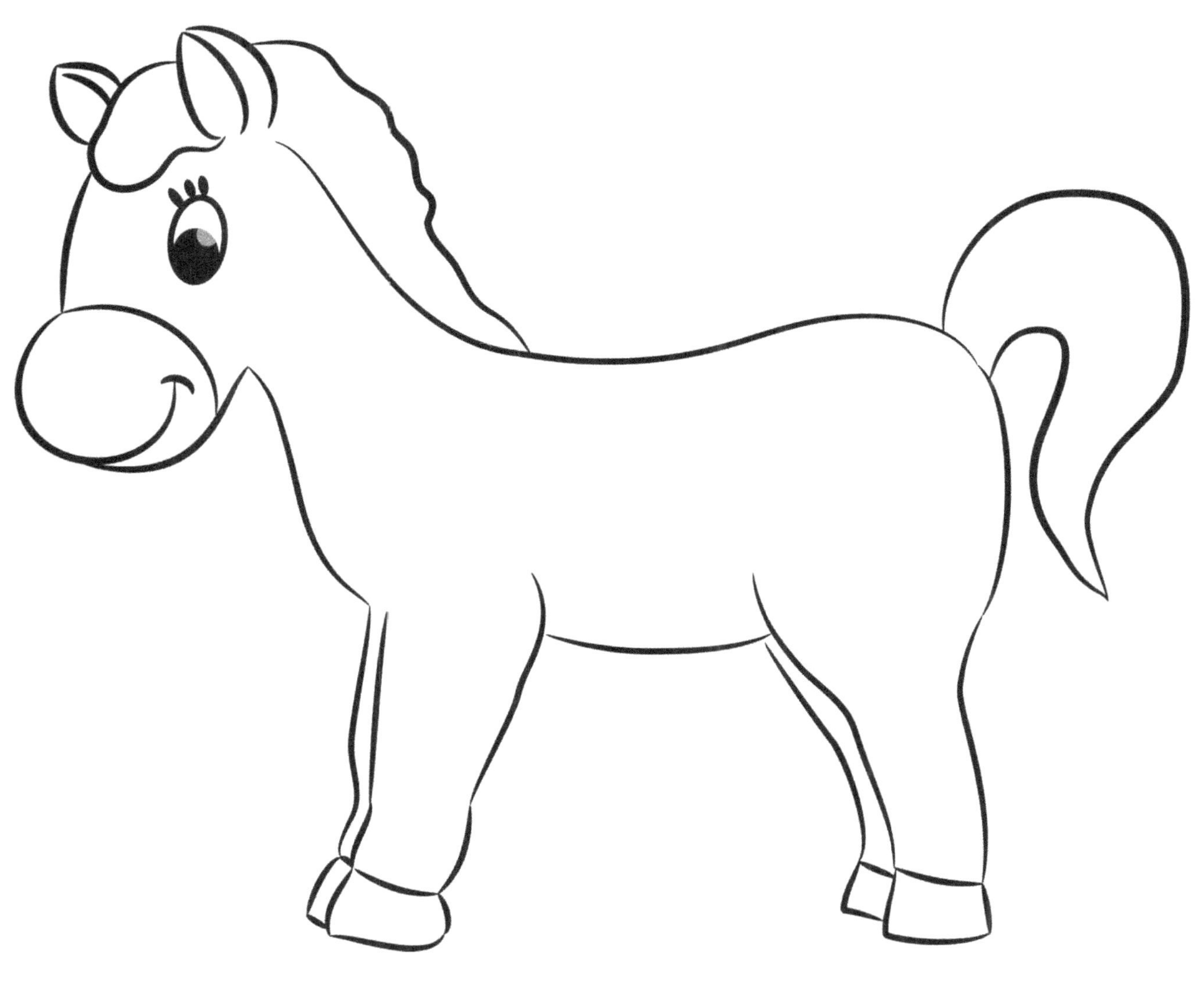

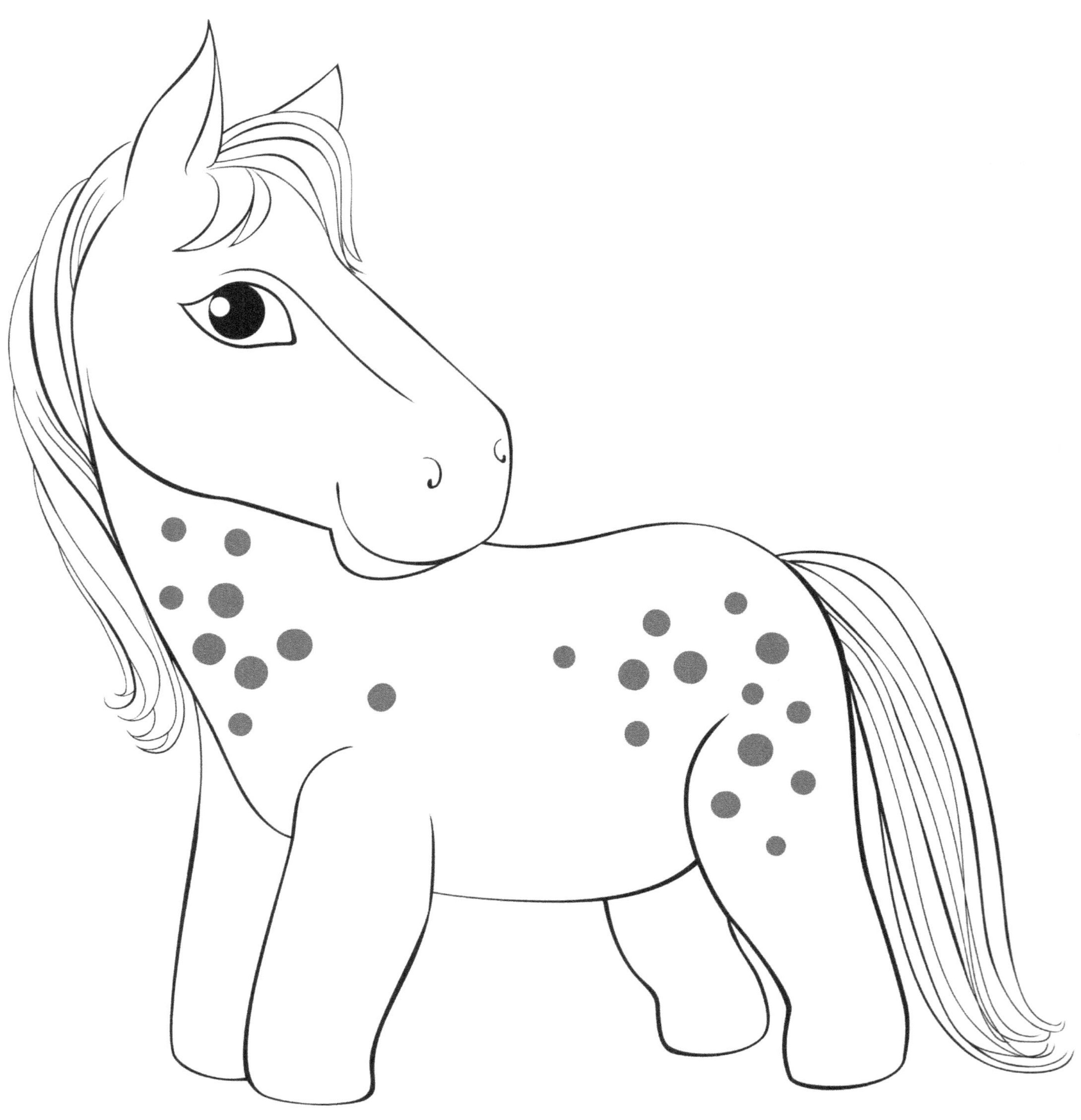

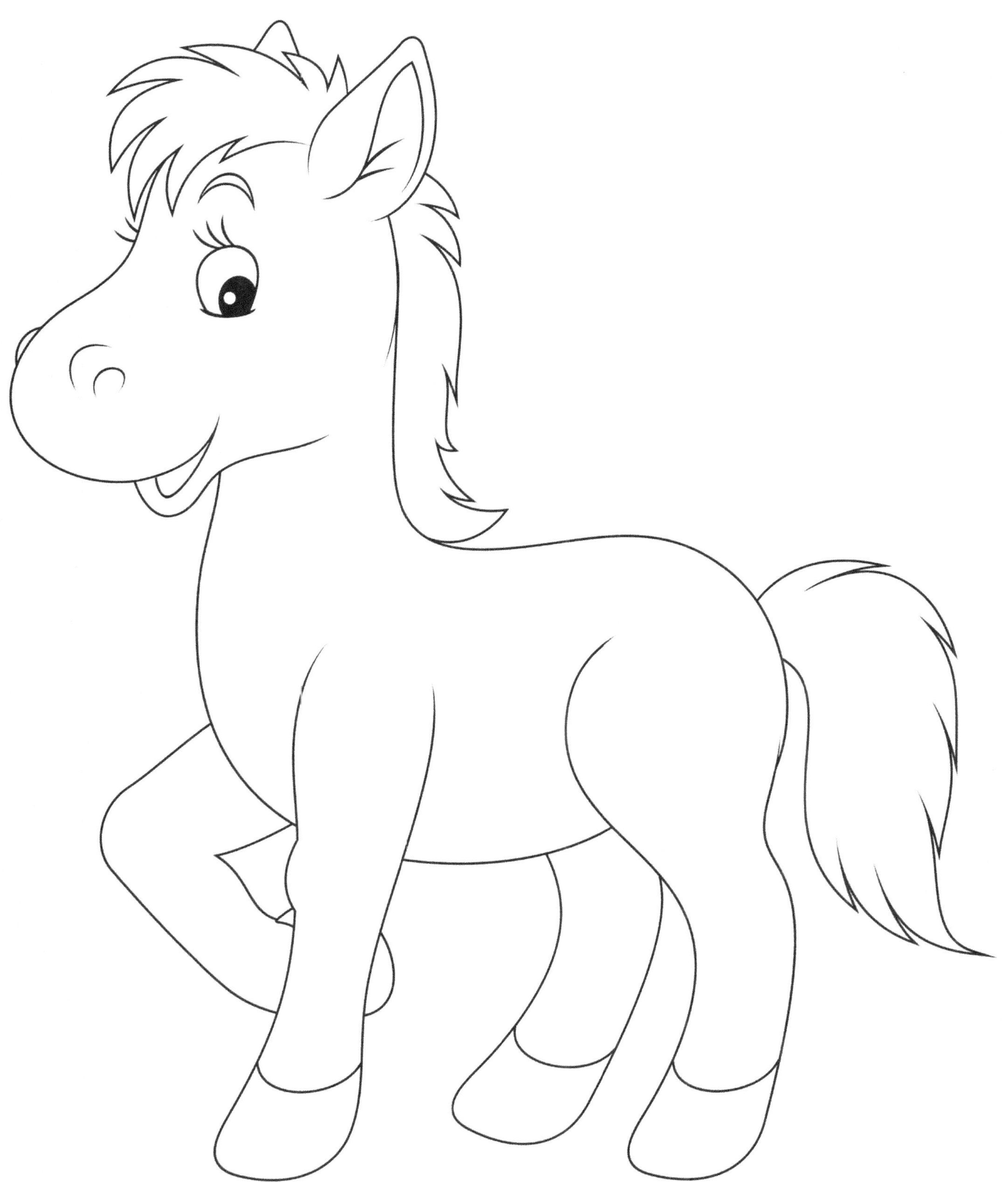

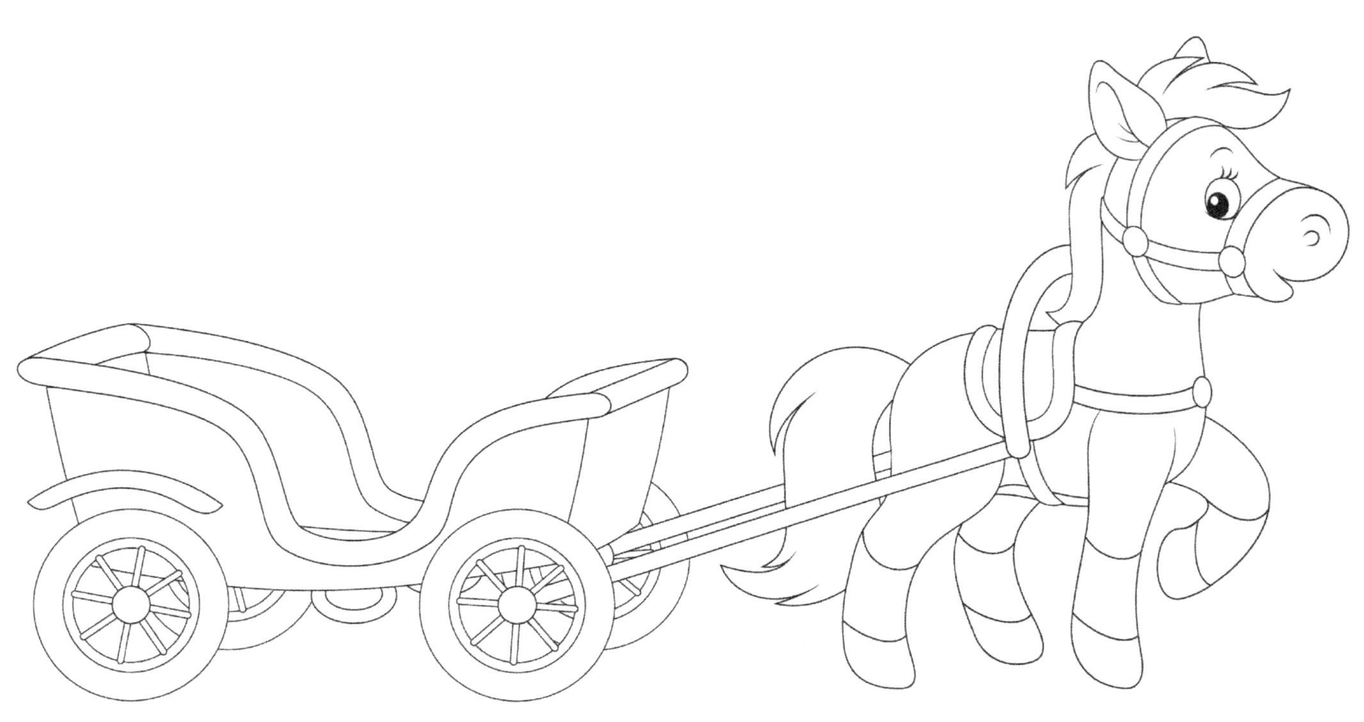

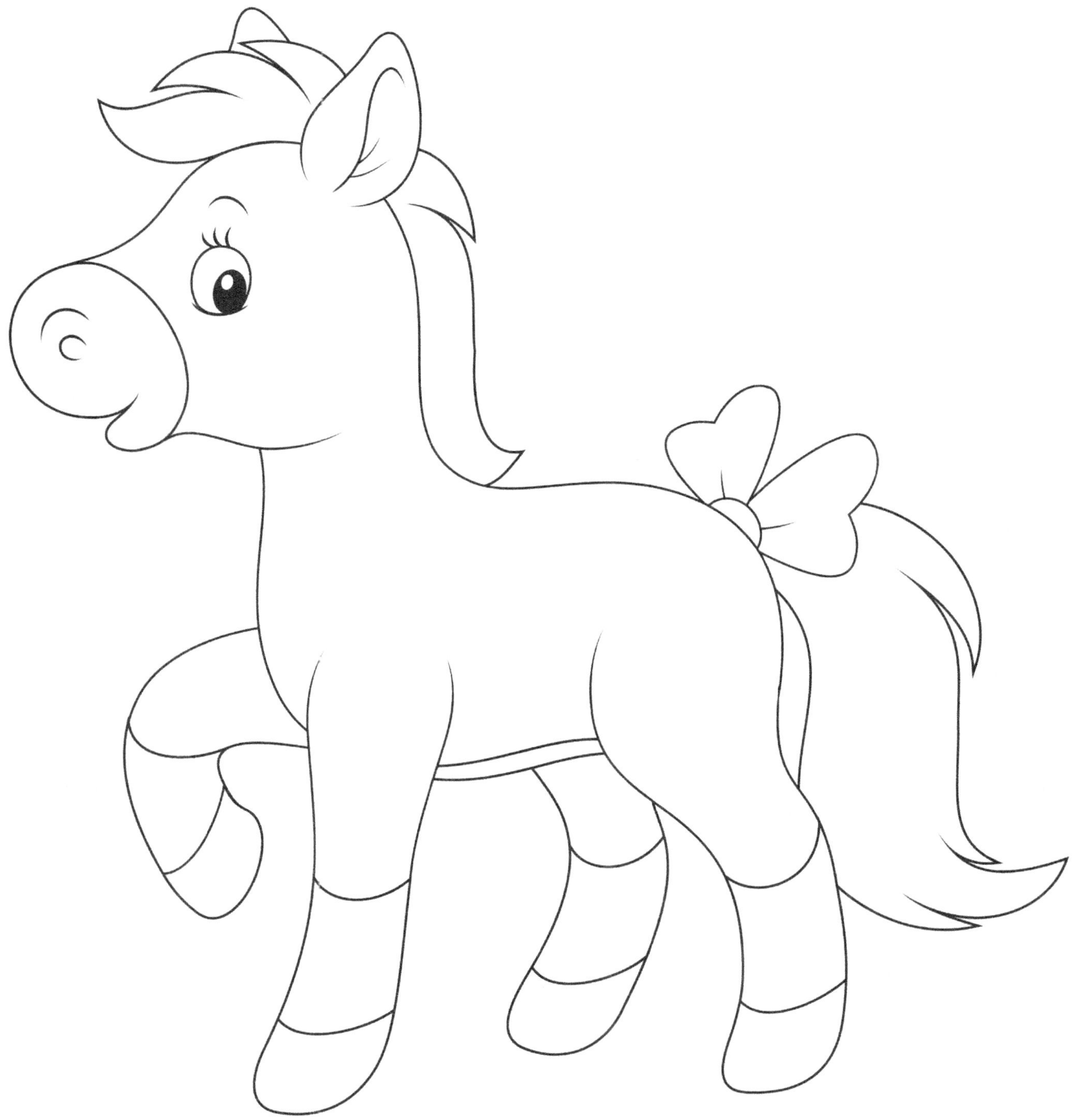

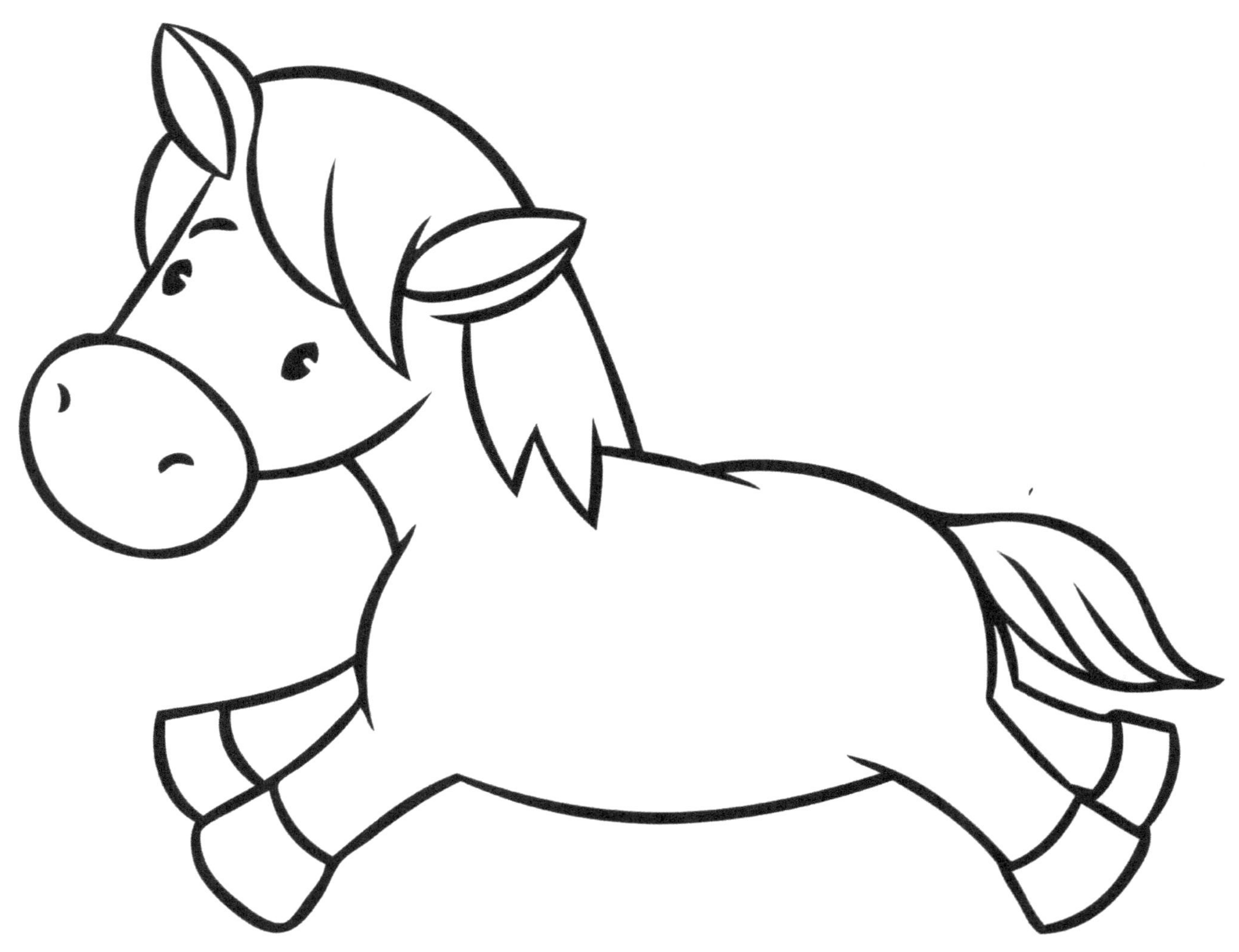

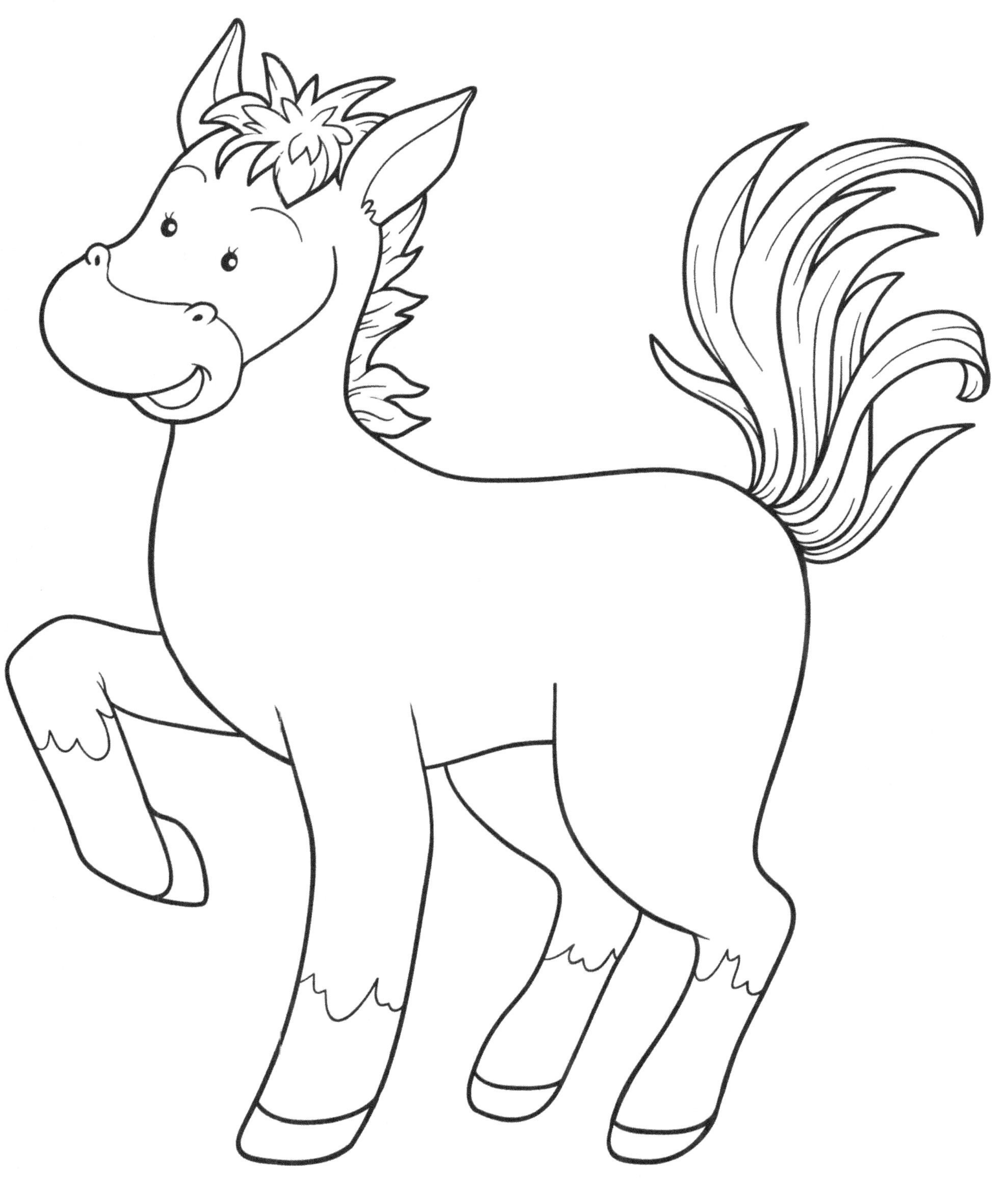

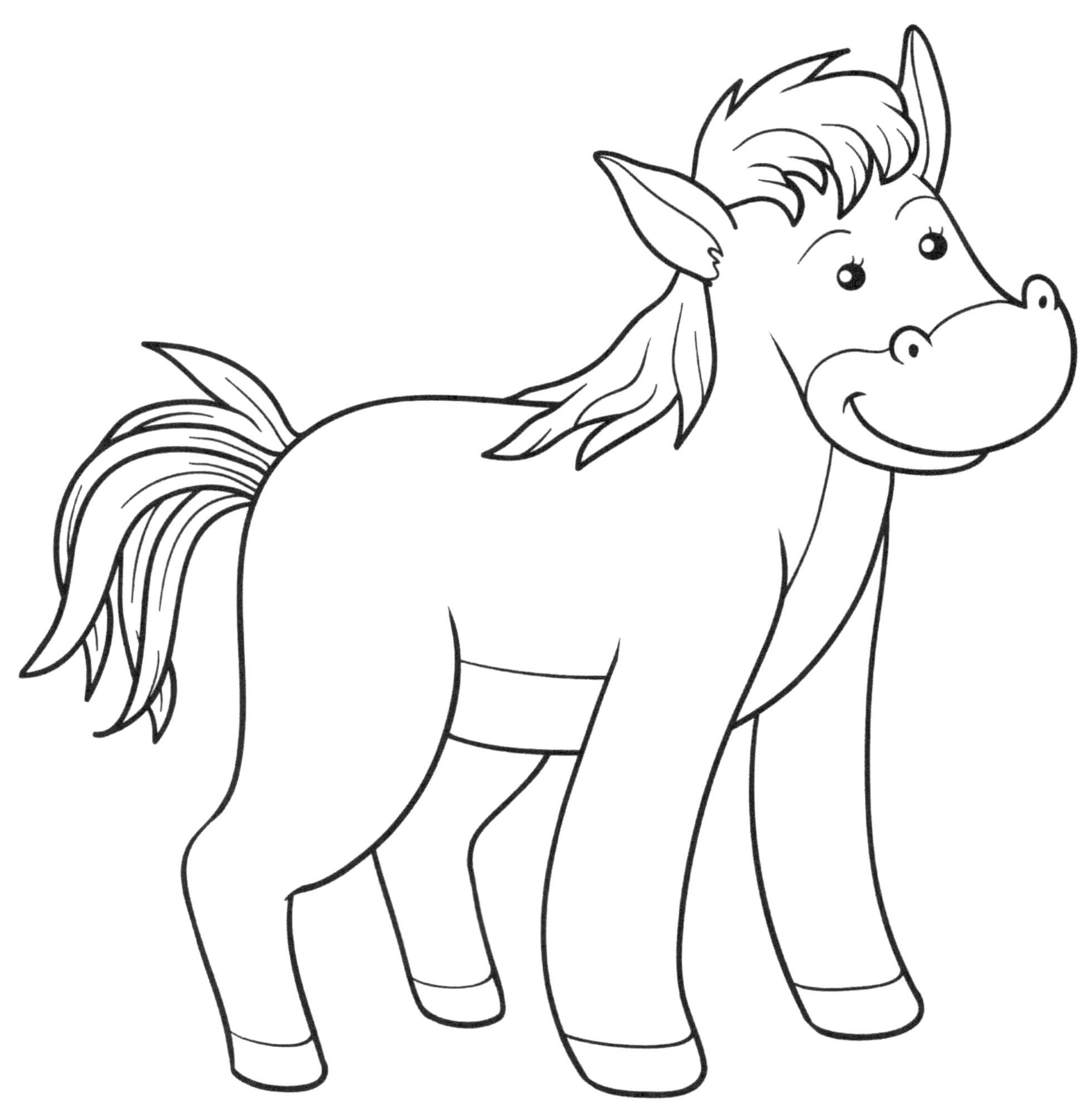

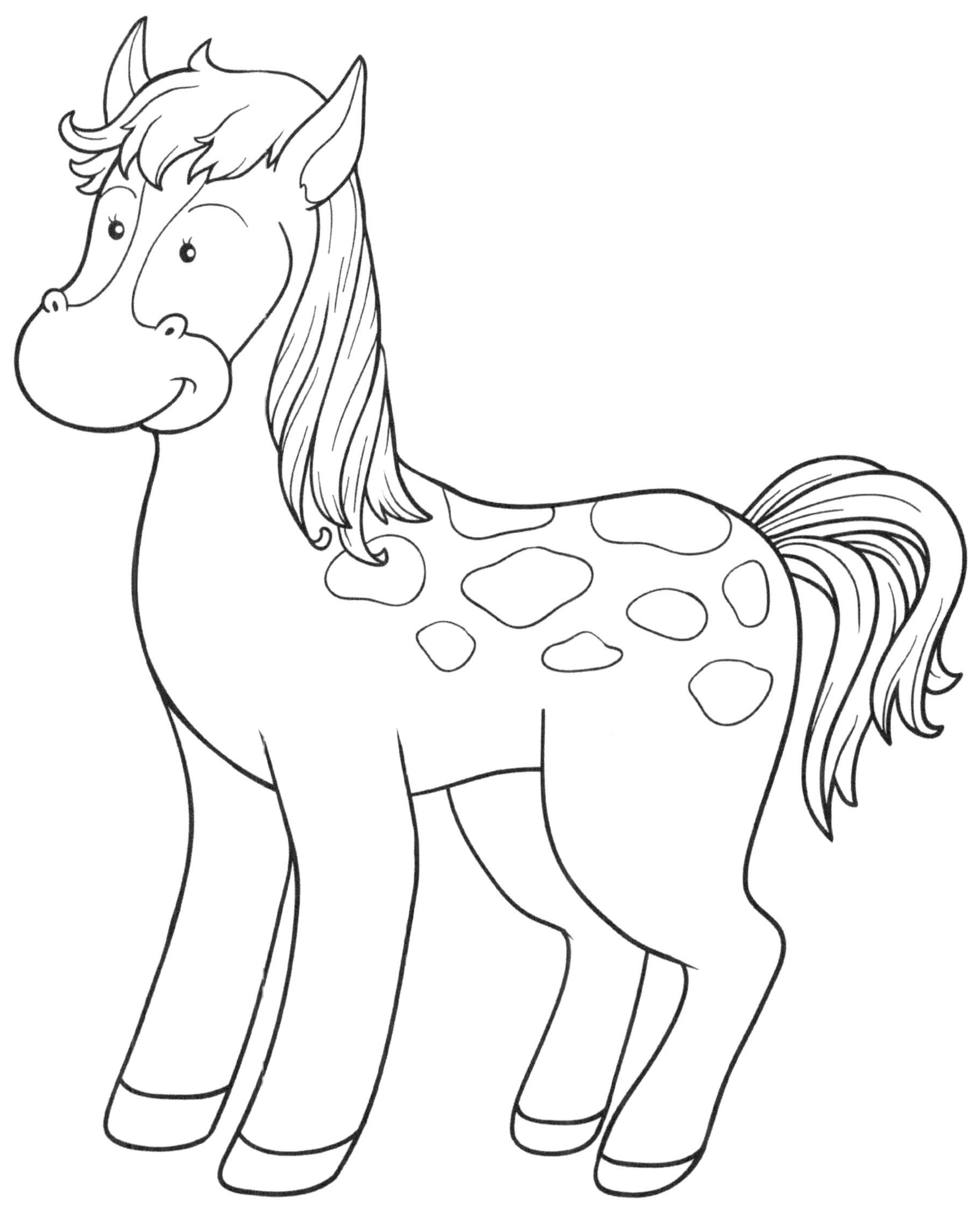

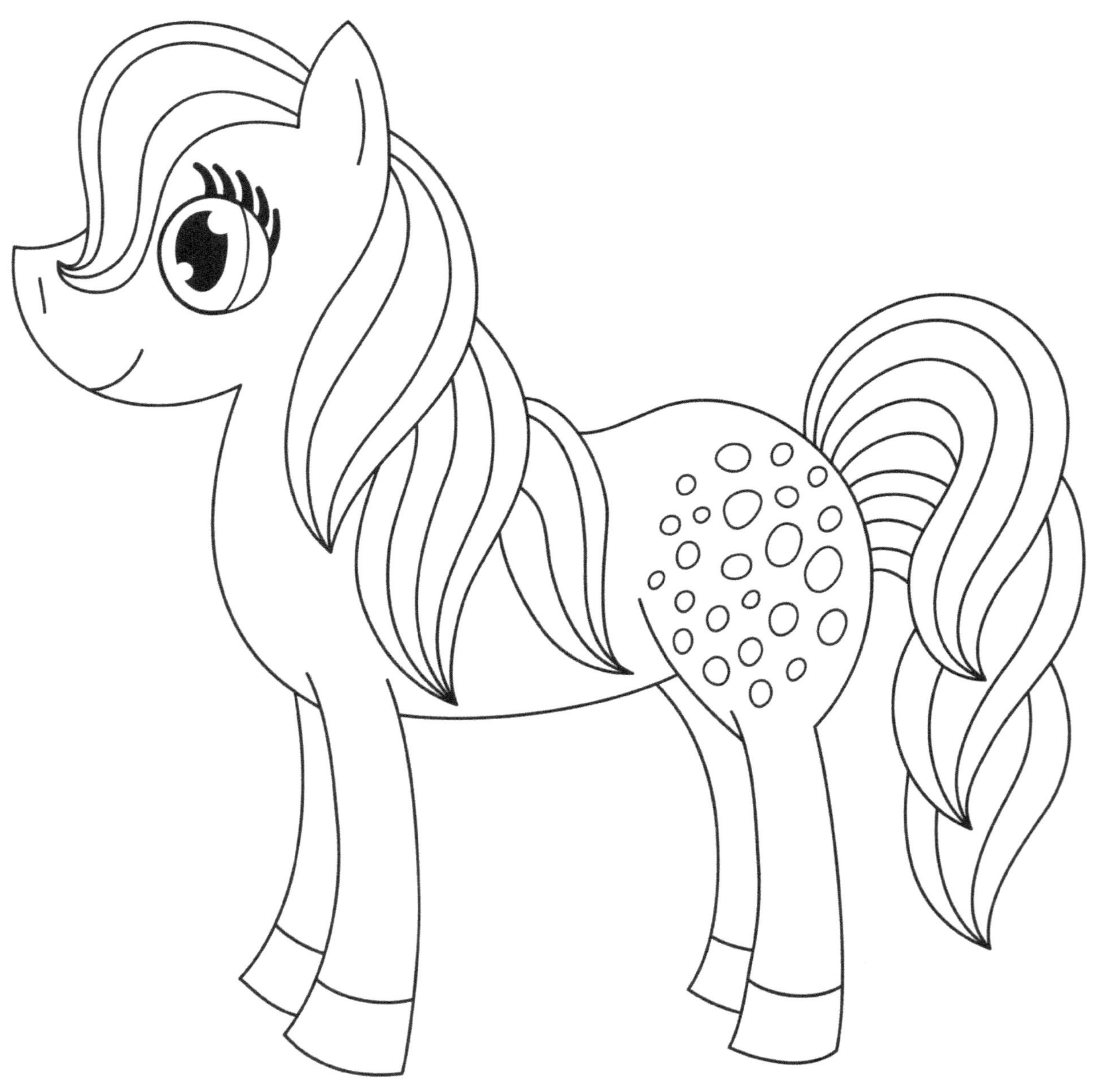

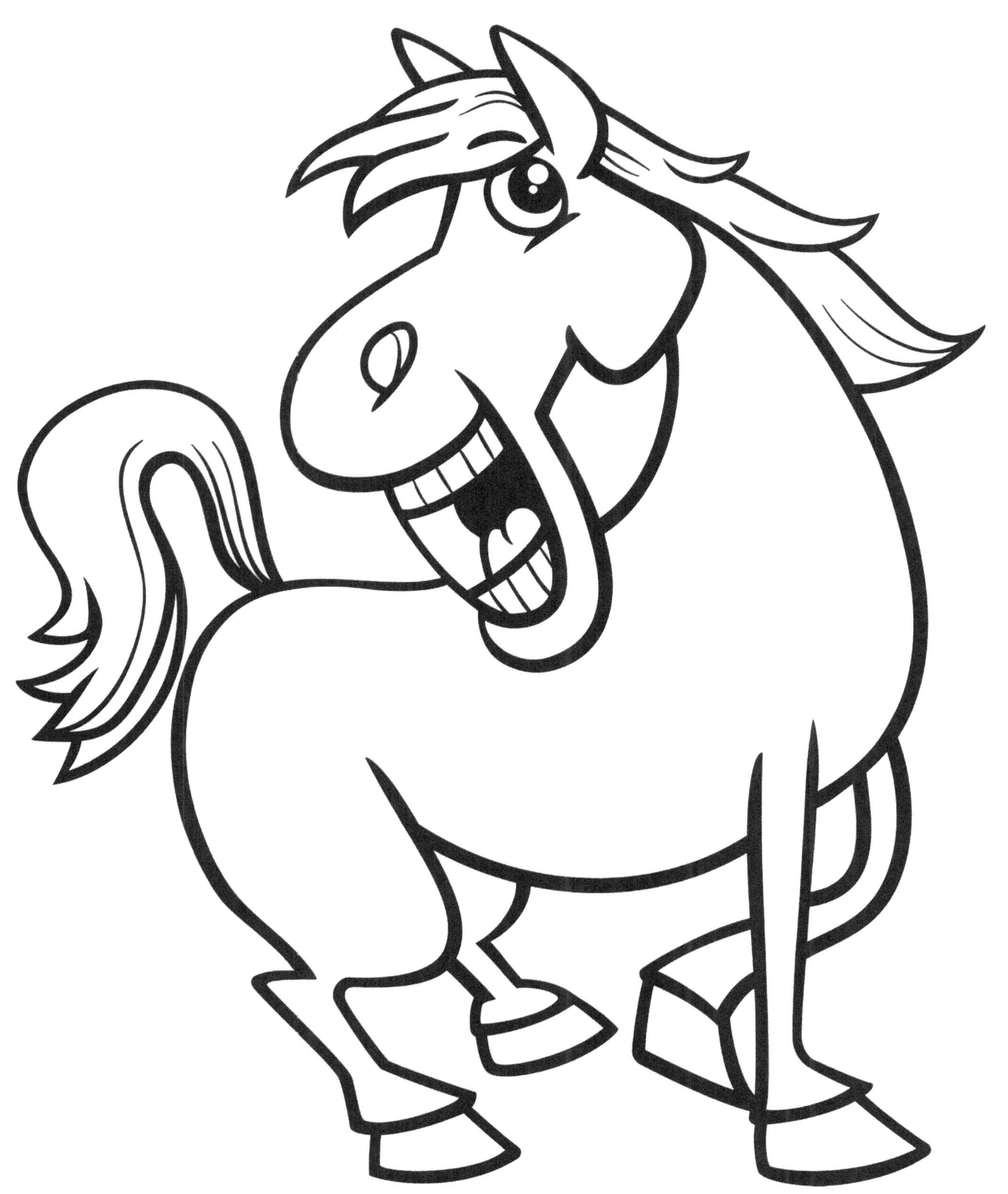

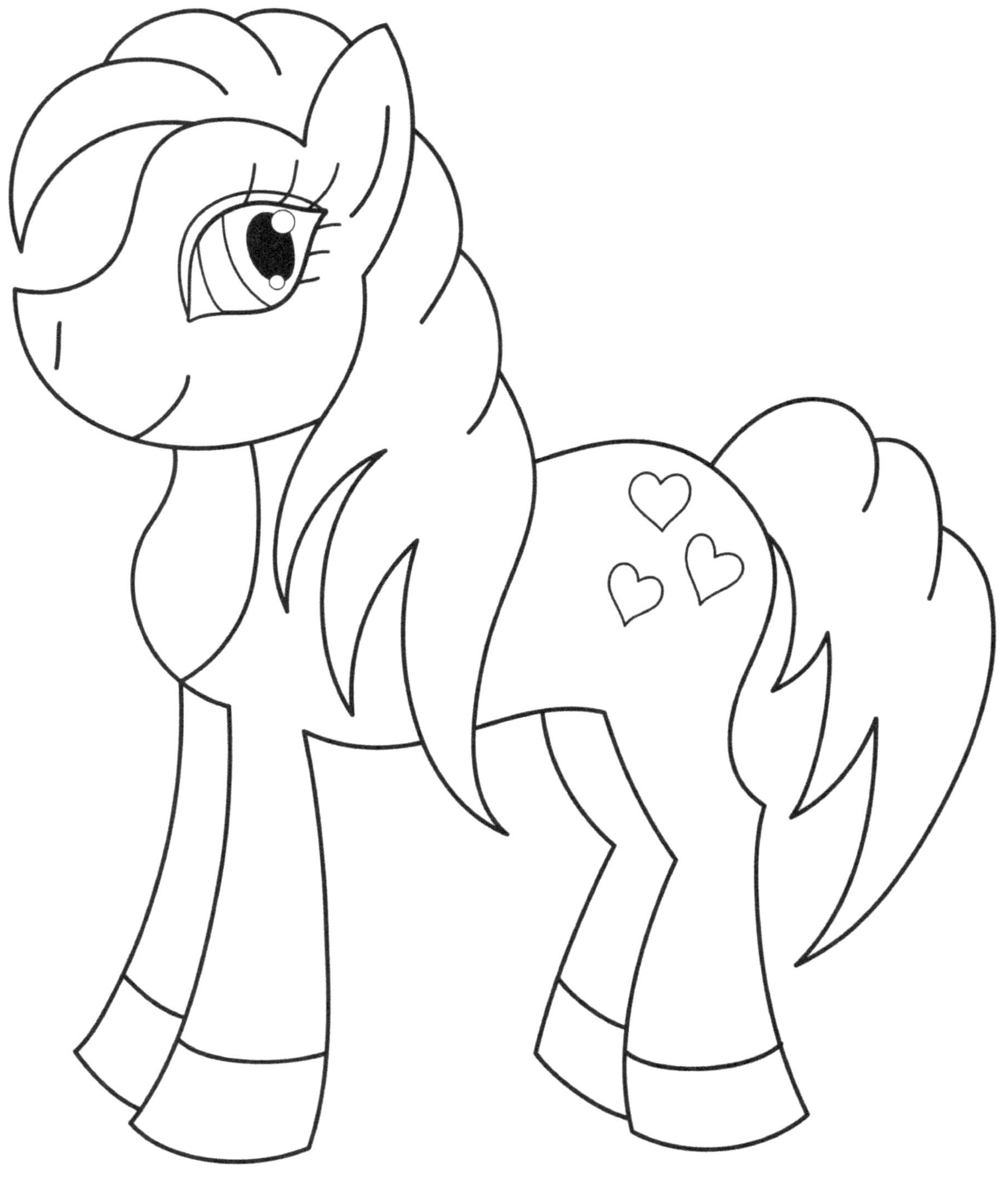

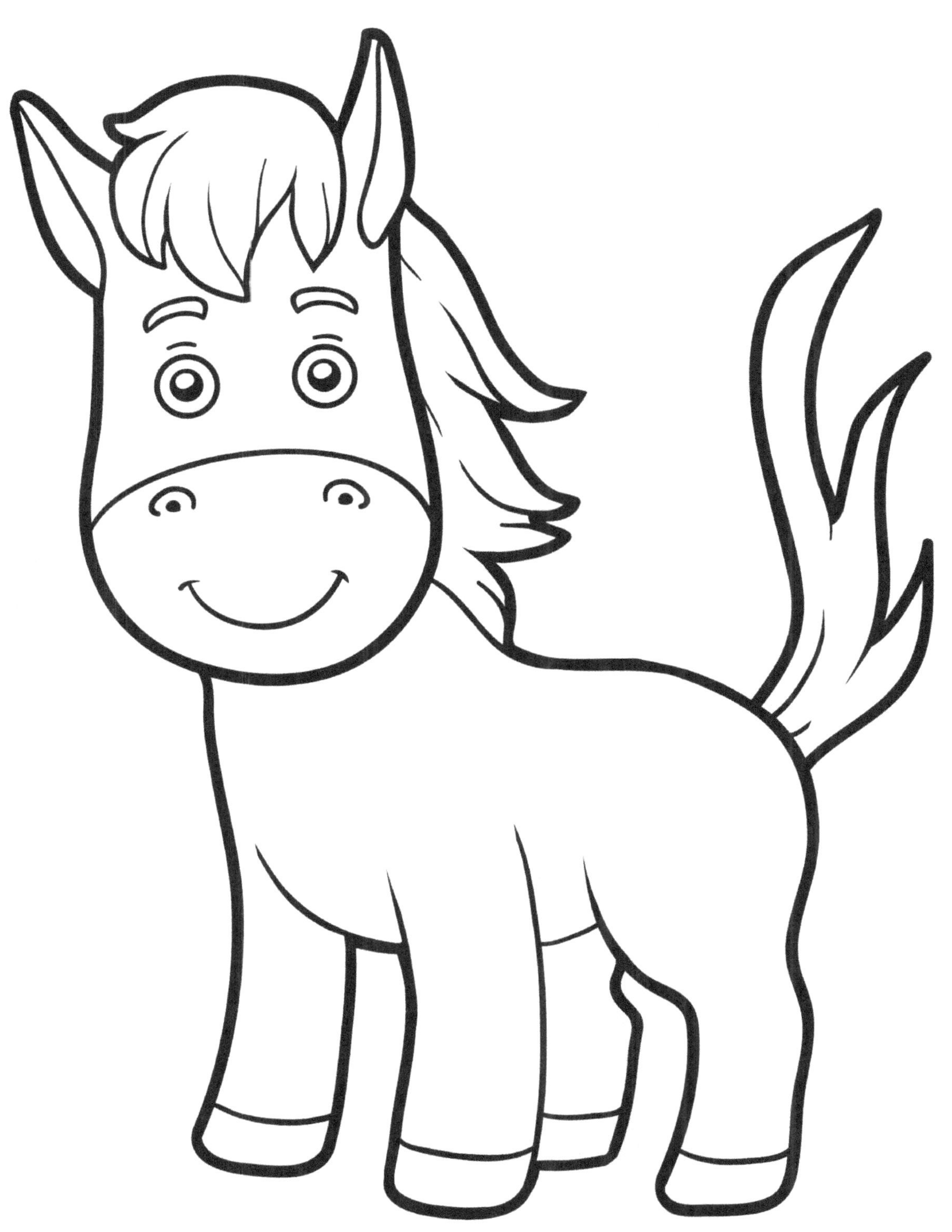

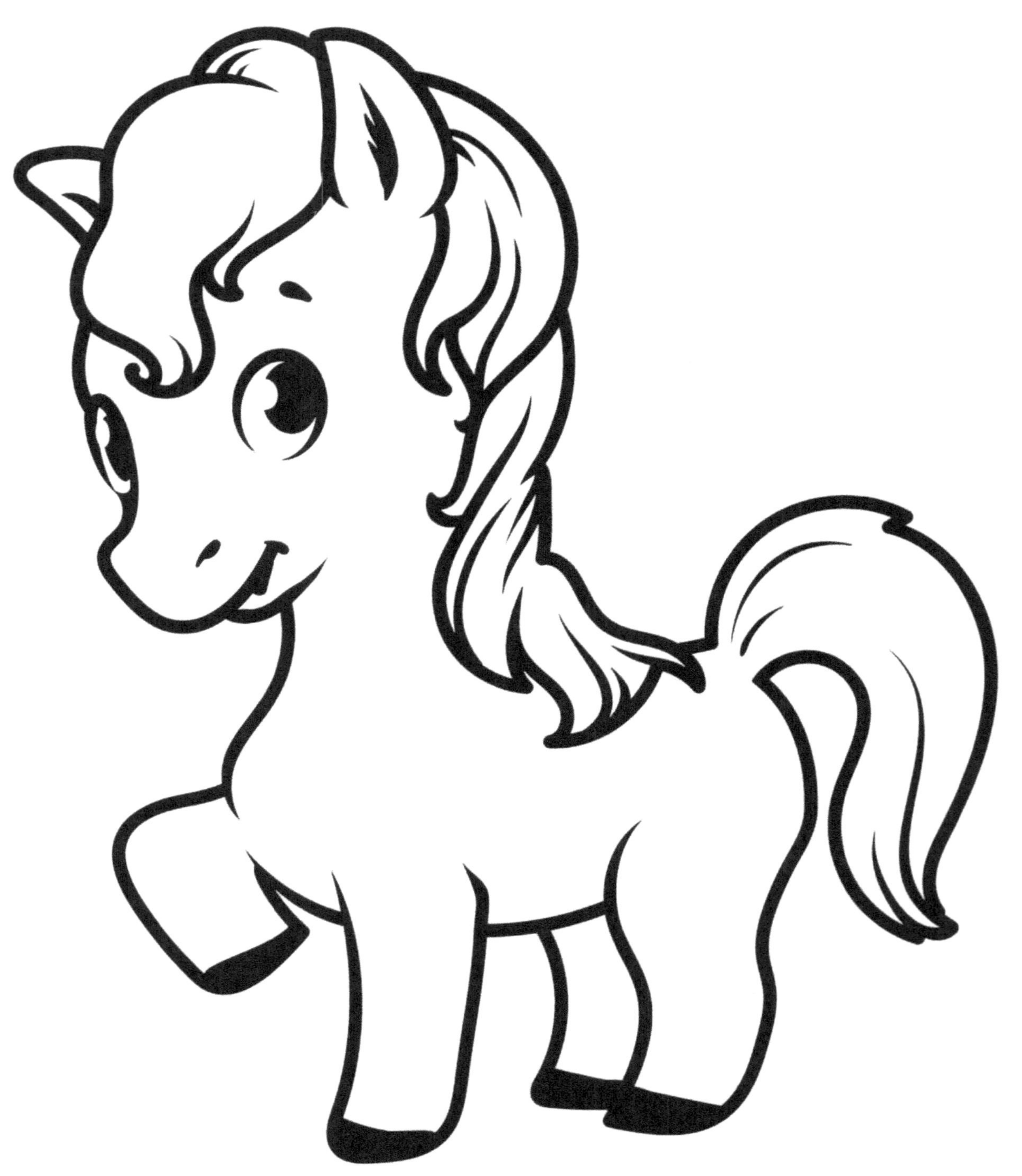

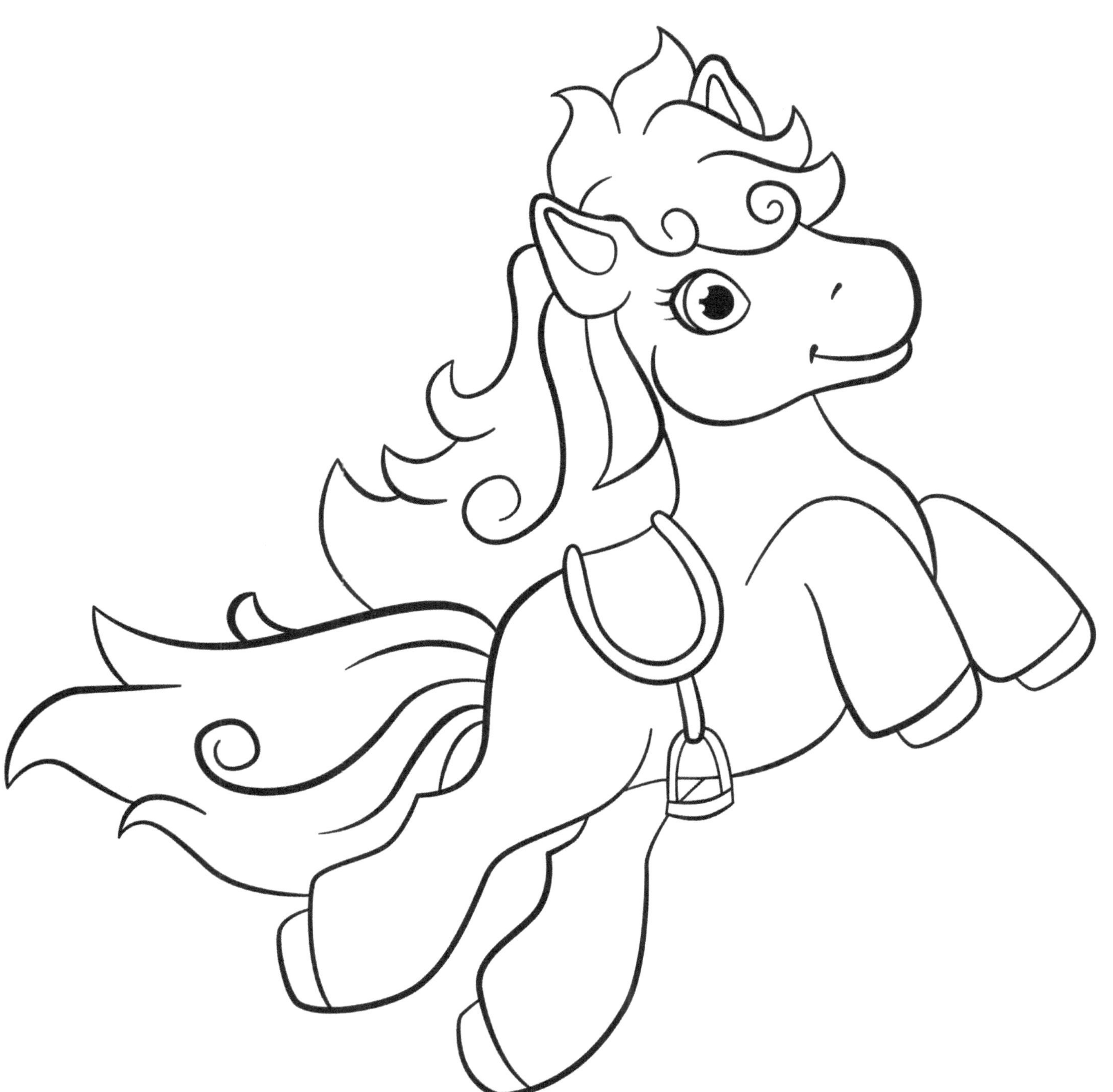

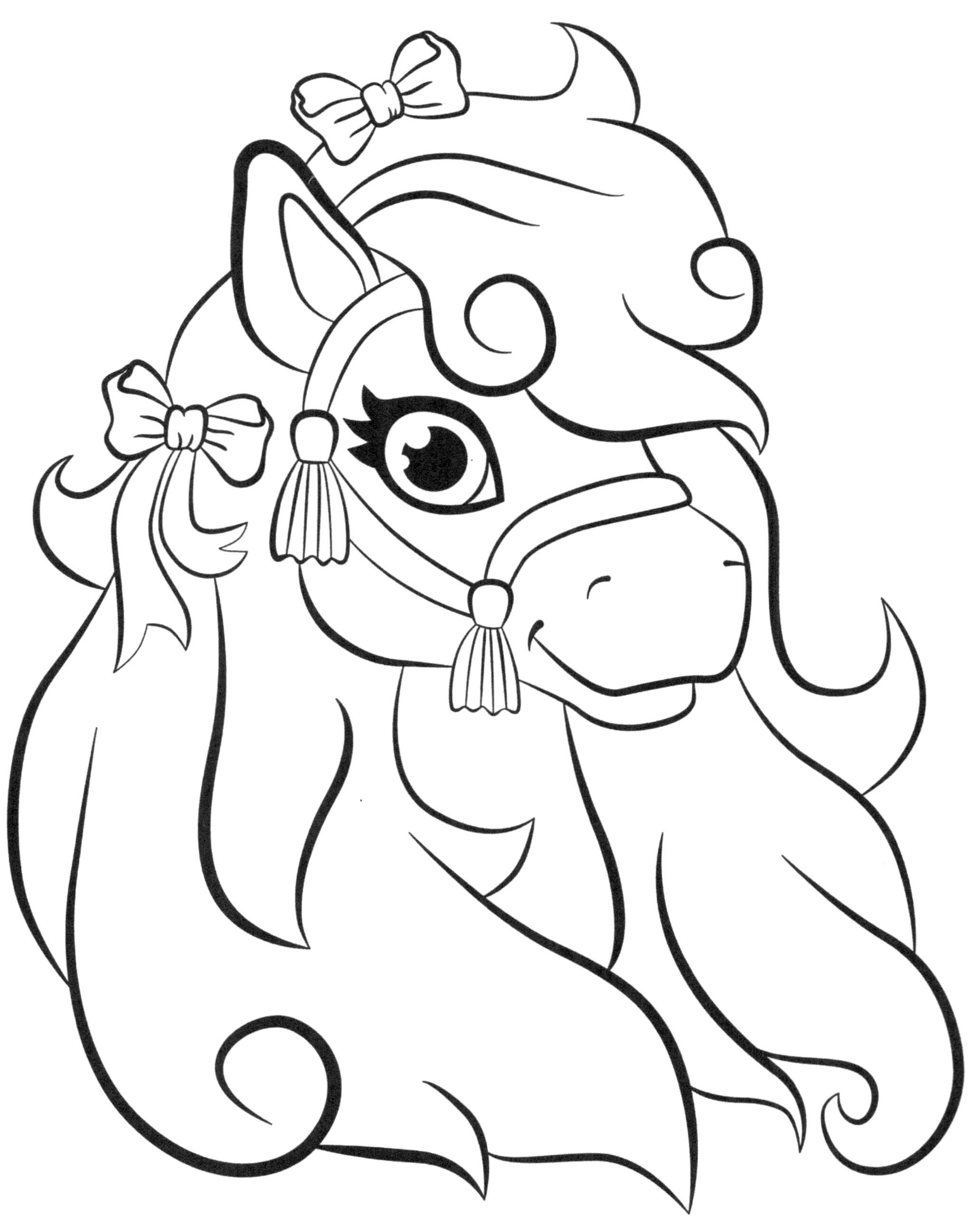

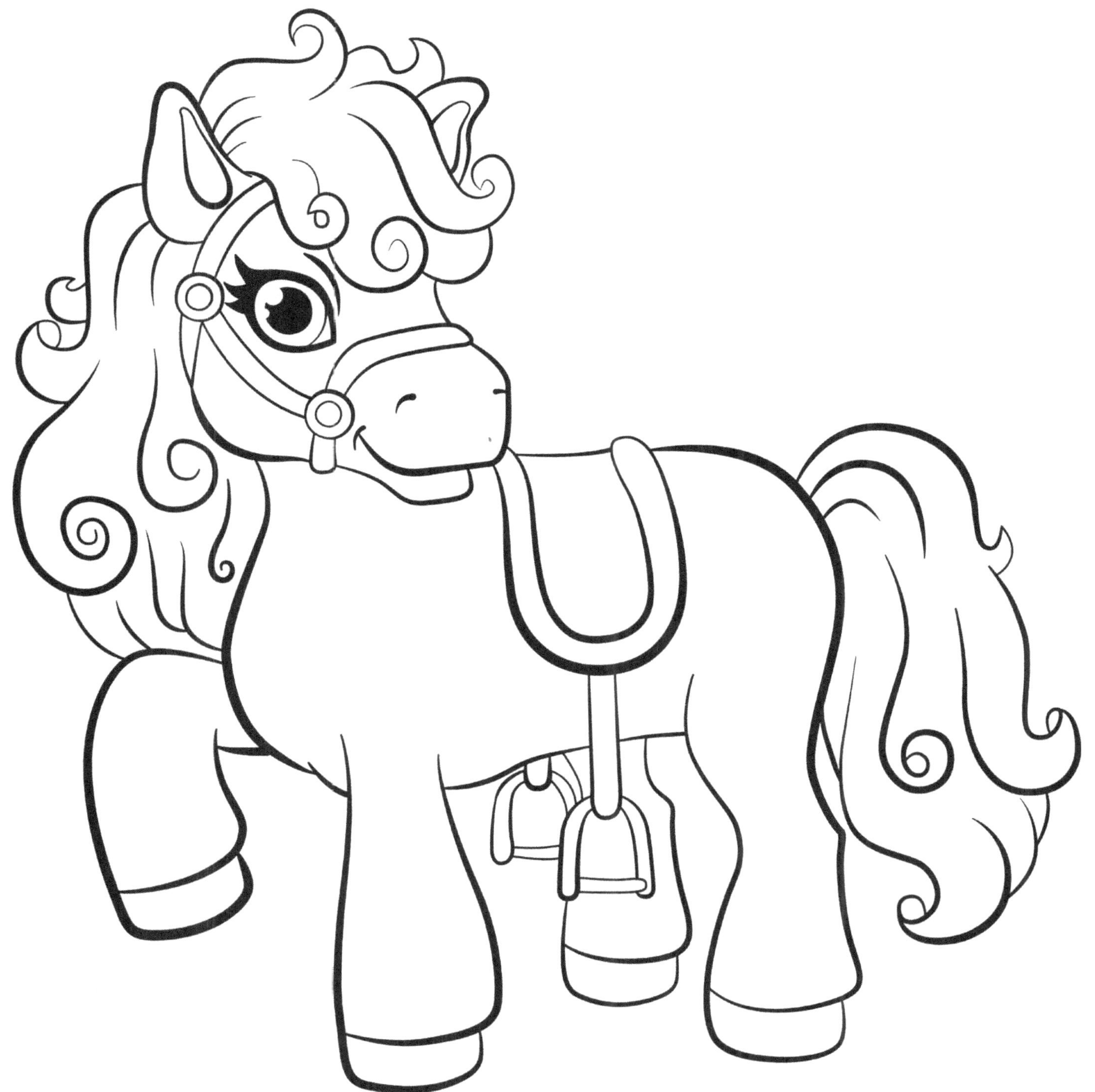

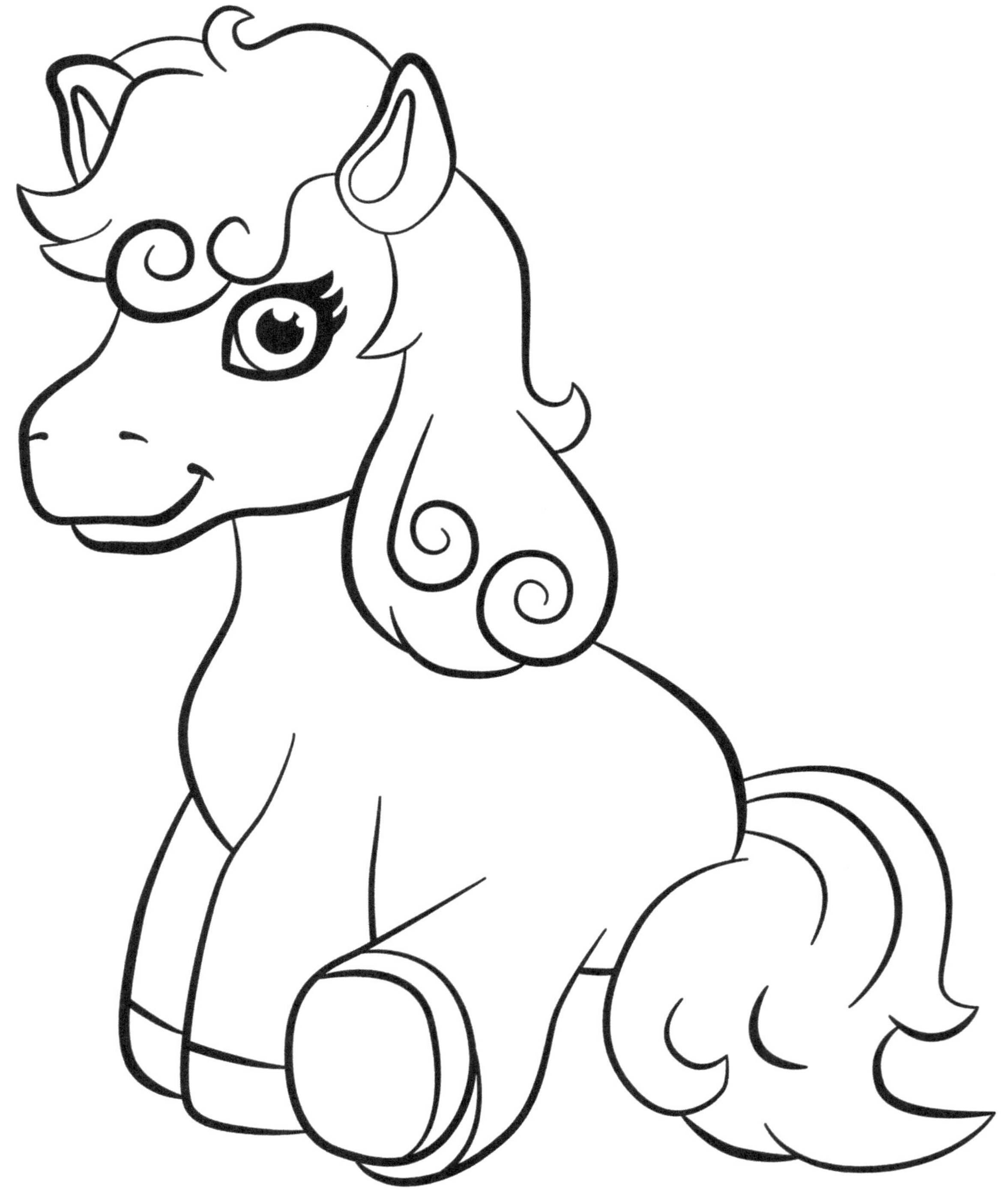

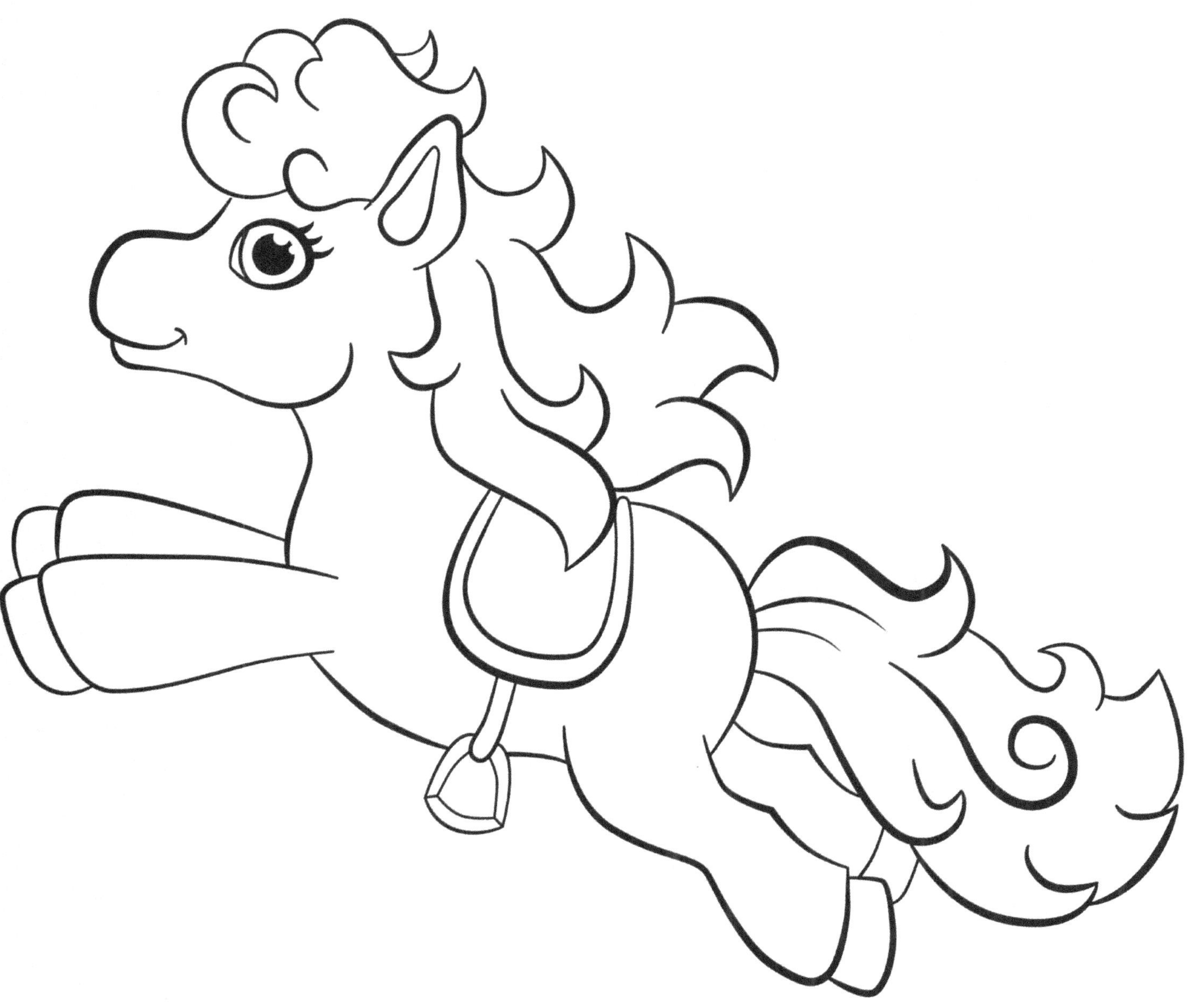

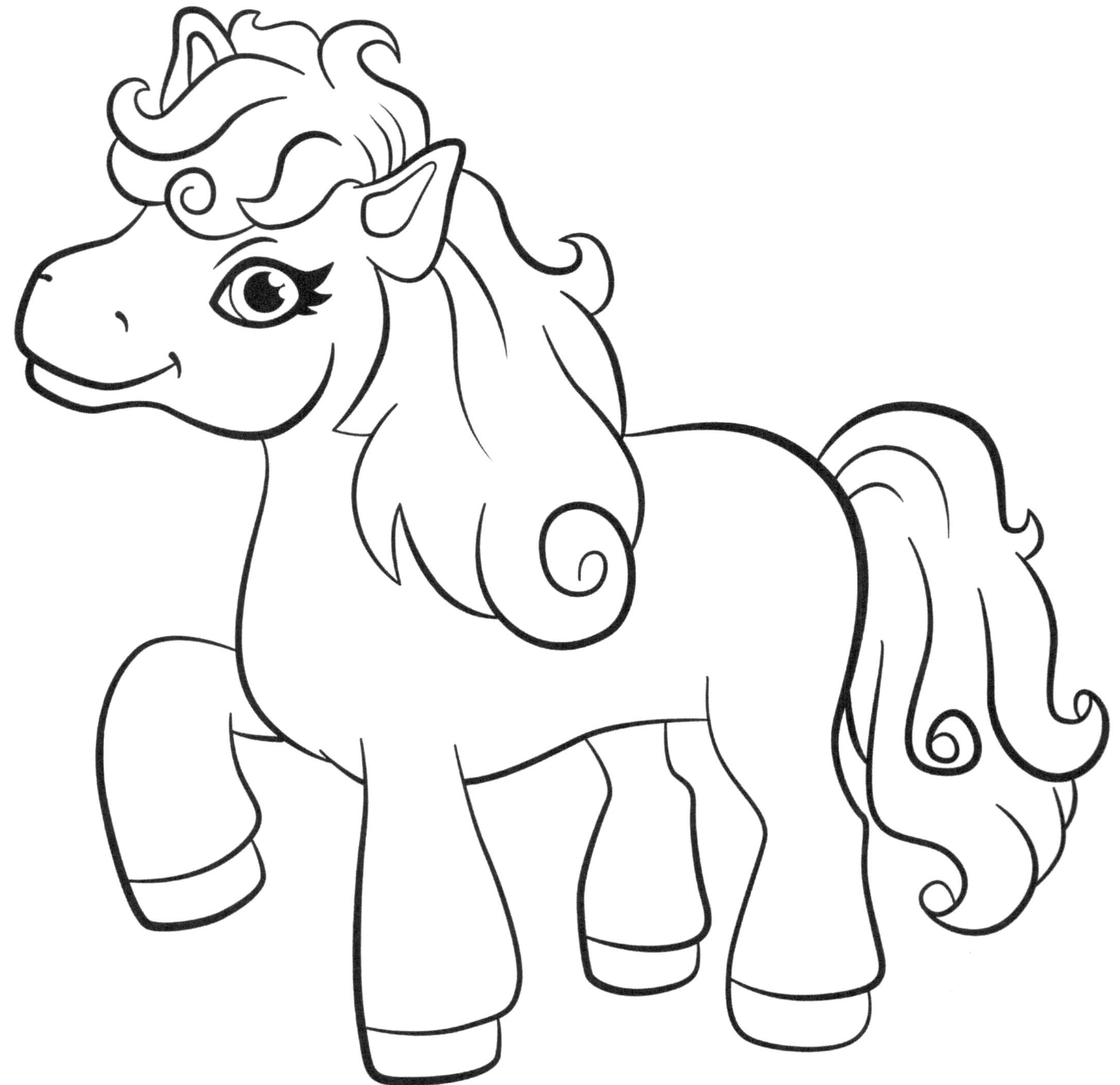

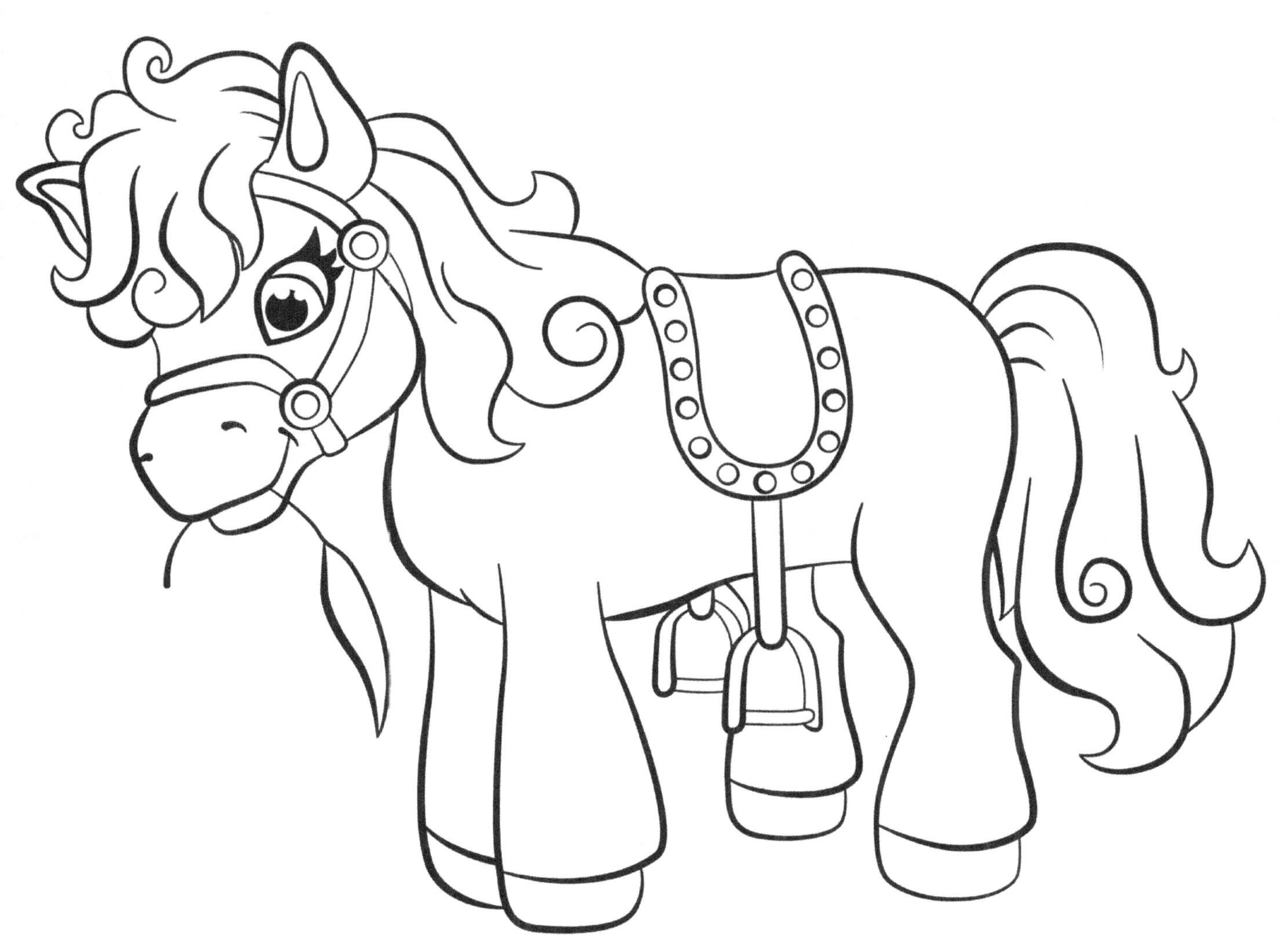

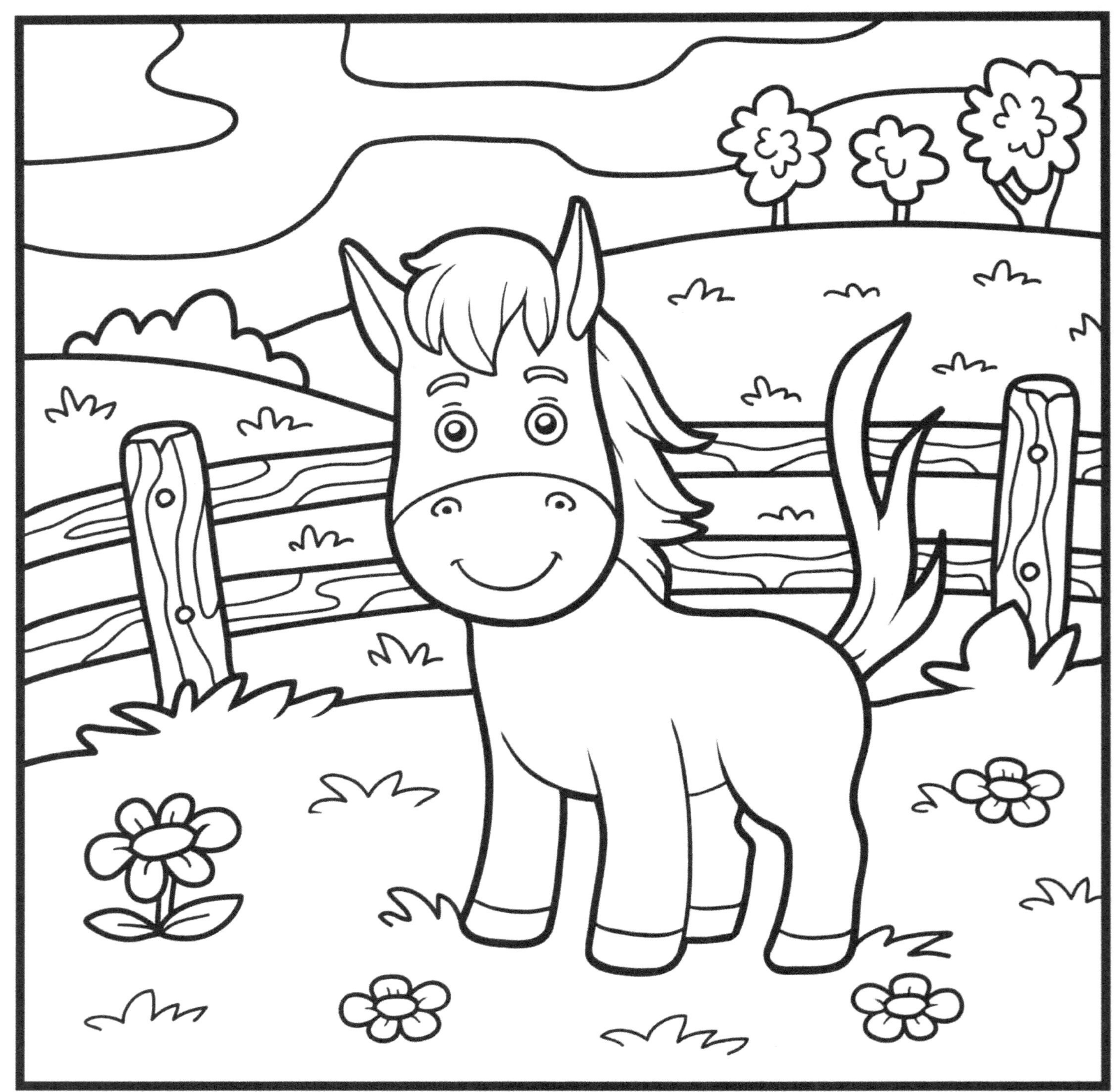